YOU ARE
WONDERFUL!

YOU ARE
WONDERFUL!

ROBERT
SCHULLER

The C.R. Gibson Company
Norwalk, Connecticut 06856

Grateful appreciation is expressed to Word Books
for permission to excerpt material that originally
appeared in THE BE (HAPPY) ATTITUDES,
copyright © 1985 by Robert H. Schuller, published
by Word Books and for material excerpted from
SELF ESTEEM, copyright © 1982 by Robert H.
Schuller, published by Word Books.

Published by the C. R. Gibson Company
Norwalk, Connecticut 06856
Copyright © 1987 by Word Books
Printed in the United States of America
ISBN 0-8378-1827-3

For information contact:
Word Books
4800 W. Waco Drive
Waco, Texas 76796

YOU ARE WONDERFUL BECAUSE...

YOU ARE A BELOVED CHILD OF GOD!

OUR INHERITANCE

What is the basic problem in our world today? Many human beings don't realize who they are. And if we don't know who we are and where we have come from, we will never become what we were meant to be. For an identity crisis will generate a self-acceptance crisis! But if we perceive ourselves as children of God, then He is our Father. We have an inheritance waiting for us. God has been waiting to find us.

A SOLID FOUNDATION

I know many Southern Californians who seem to forget the importance of a foundation when it comes to buying a house. Some of the first questions they ask are, "What kind of a view does it have?" "What is the architectural style?" "Does it have a shake roof?" "Are there any schools nearby?" "What is the resale value?" But they ignore the most important questions, "Is the ground solid?" "Will the house stand?" So there are tragedies every year when the earth gives way and expensive homes crumble because the most important factor was missing— a solid foundation.

If we have a problem in our life today; if something is missing emotionally, if there is something lacking deep in our soul, let us begin by asking ourselves the most basic question: "Do I have a positive sense of self-respect or self-esteem?" This is an important question because if there can be one generalized description of the human predicament in the world today, it would be the lack of self-esteem in human beings. Until we are conscious of our belonging to the family of God we will experience an identity crisis which will create a self-esteem crisis.

GOD'S PROVIDENCE

I met Eric Sloane one week when I was in
New York City, making television appear-
ances. I had an hour between appoint-
ments and I said to my driver, "How far is
it to the Armand Hammer Galleries?"

"Oh," he said, "not far." So we
stopped in the galleries. In one area was a
one-man show by Eric Sloane. The walls
were covered with beautiful paintings of
sky and covered American bridges.

One customer was looking at a beautiful painting. He looked at me, and whis-
pered to his wife. I knew what they were
saying, so I walked over and said hello.

They said, "Oh, Dr. Schuller. We
watch you every week." Then they
turned to the paintings on the wall. "Isn't
his work gorgeous?'

"Yes!"

They said, "It's too bad you weren't
here last night, at the opening, because
Eric Sloane himself was here."

Just then the door opened. How provi-
dential could it be? The couple I had been
talking to said, "Oh, here he comes."

I watched a man walk in—ramrod
straight, silver-haired. I spotted dimples
and twinkles in the eye, a beautiful blue
bow tie, a white shirt, and a double-
breasted wool overcoat.

He greeted the customer, who led him over to me. As Mr. Sloane came close, he said, "Dr. Schuller, you look just like you do on television."

He was a friend. He said, "I'll tell you why I've loved your ministry, Dr. Schuller." Then he told me this story:

"I was a very young man when I inherited a million dollars in cash from my father. You wouldn't believe how quickly I spent it all! I woke up one Sunday morning and realized I did not have one dollar left. I was terribly depressed. My inheritance was gone, my father was dead, and I had nothing. I went into a little church—although I was not really very religious—and I heard the minister say, 'God's providence is your inheritance.'

"He didn't know about me.

"But the minister continued, 'God will provide, no matter how bankrupt you are. But you have to trust Him and turn your whole life over to Him.'

"At that time I was just a sign painter. But I took my brush, and underneath my easel I wrote the words, *God's providence is my inheritance.* Once I put that on my easel, my whole life changed."

He continued, "I couldn't be more successful than I am today."

I said, "Would you like to be my guest on *The Hour of Power* some Sunday?"

He enthusiastically replied, "I'd love to be."

That was on Monday. Imagine my shock when I heard three days later that Eric Sloane had died.

"God's providence is my inheritance." Eric Sloane claimed it. And the same inheritance is waiting for you and me. All we have to do is claim it.

THE SELF-ESTEEM PRAYER

The Lord's Prayer clears the way for a healthy theology of self-esteem, for it deals with the classic negative emotions that destroy our self-dignity. The Lord's Prayer offers Christ's positive solution from these six basic, negative emotions that infect and affect our self-worth:

1) Inferiority:
"Our Father who are in heaven,
Hallowed be thy name."

2) Depression:
"Thy kingdom come, Thy will be done,
On earth as it is in heaven."

3) Anxiety:
"Give us this day our daily bread;"

4) Guilt:
"And forgive us our debts,"

5) Resentment:
"As we also have forgiven our debtors;"

6) Fear:
"And lead us not into temptation,
But deliver us from evil."

Our compulsion to excellence is driven by our spiritual self-esteem. "I am God's child entrusted with God's idea so I must excel! I must not settle for mediocrity." This pursuit of excellence is fantastic—but potentially dangerous if it leads to unrealistic perfectionism. Perfectionism is unrealistic excellence which produces guilt. How do we solve this

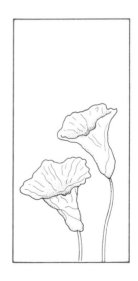

problem? How do we avoid the guilt of perfectionism without defusing the drive to excellence? The answer: "By inserting the concept of forgiveness!" So God dropped into its proper place in this prayer the next healing sentence: "Forgive us our debts as we forgive our debtors."

"I AM LOVED NO MATTER WHAT"

The meek are patient. And the patient will inherit the earth. A modern-day example of patience and the reward it brings is a young lady whom I have grown to respect and admire. Her name is Lisa Welchel. Many of you know her as Blair, the snobby rich girl on the television series, *The Facts of Life*.

Lisa got her start when she was seven years old. She read that auditions were being held for the Mickey Mouse Club, so she wrote and asked if she could audition. She was told that the auditions had already been held and the show had been cast. But Lisa didn't quit. She wrote lots and lots of letters. Her final letter said, "I'm a Christian, and I feel that Disney is the only place I can work right now because the context of other shows is not what I could represent. I would really appreciate a chance to audition. I would be willing to fly myself out there." Disney agreed to give Lisa a chance. They liked her and she got the part. From there, she got the part of Blair, who is really very different from Lisa.

Lisa is a charming, delightful girl who lives and works in Hollywood, which many would say is a difficult if not impossible place for a beautiful, young, single girl to retain old-fashioned values and Christian behavior. I asked Lisa about this, and here's what she said: "Well, you know, I feel that all the values the Lord has laid down for us are really for our own benefit. And if we think that we want to do something contrary to those values, well, that's fine, but we're only going to be hurting ourselves if we give in. God knows the future, and He knows why He set down certain rules. I feel that the Lord is just. Like He says, He's our Father and He's looking out for us. So long as I can remember that God's rules are only for my good and for my own happiness, and that He knows better than I do, then they are easy to adhere to."

Lisa knows the secret to happiness. She is so bubbly, so enthusiastic. I asked her, "Lisa, where do you get your enthusiasm, your love for life?" Her answer was psychologically and theologically sound. She said, "It's from knowing that I am loved no matter what, and that I don't have to perform and I don't have to be a good person. I don't even have to follow the Lord's laws to be loved. It's just total grace and it's all mercy. It's knowing that I'm loved just because He created me. So if I blow it, I blow it, but Jesus is still standing here with open arms. And if I do good He's standing there to commend me."

HONOR HIS FAMILY!

God's name is glorified when His children are living honorable and glorious lives. God's glory is diminished as long as any of His children remain lost in shame, falling short of the pride and glory they should enjoy as princes and princesses of heaven. The Christian faith and life is a gospel designed to glorify human beings for the greater glory of God.

For example, the father of a family is honored and his name is honored as each of the children rise to the challenges of personal achievement—morally, spiritually, and professionally. But if just one child rejects the high call to honorable living as becomes the family heritage, the father and the family's glory is diminished.

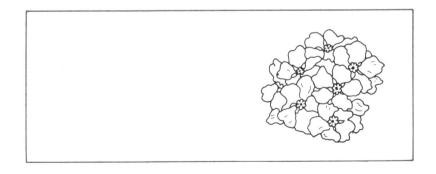

A NOBLE PATH

When we know that we are born to be children of God, we will be inspired to choose the noble path. When we have a tremendous sense of self-respect, we don't stoop to crime. It's beneath our dignity. When we have a consciousness that we belong to the family of God, we develop the healing, helpful, and divine sense of righteous pride. It will not be a sinful pride; it will be a redemptive pride.

What is our Lord's greatest passion for His church today? I believe that He wants His followers to respect themselves as equal children of God and to treat all other human beings with that same respect.

WHY DO PEOPLE SAY "NO"?

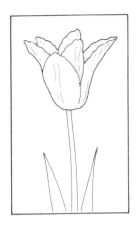

First, people say "No" to God because *they do not know any better.* There are still a lot of people who are hung up on the idea that if you really get religion, really get converted, really get saved and become a Christian, you may go off the deep end and become a little nutty or kooky or freaky. There are others who have been turned off by contact with religious hypocrites or fanatics or—worse—by joyless, negative Christians. So these people steer away from religion, never realizing what a happy life they can have when they commit their whole lives to Him.

Dwight Moody used to say, "People have just enough religion to make themselves miserable; they cannot be happy at a wild party and they are uncomfortable at a prayer meeting."

How true it is! Many people have just enough religion to be miserable, but not enough to enjoy it. And so often this is because they have no idea what Christian life is really like. Frankly, I do not blame those whose only impression of God is the negative witness some Christians give. No wonder they turn Him off! They just do not know any better.

There is a second reason why some people say "No" to God: *They do not think*

they can say "Yes" to Him. Lack of self-esteem holds them back. Their thinking is: "God is perfect and I surely know I am not; therefore, I do not think I should join up with Him." What these people don't realize is that God does not call us to be perfect; He just calls us to be willing! He doesn't expect us to be sinless, although He does expect us to say, "Lord, I am willing to try." It is far better to do something constructive imperfectly than to do nothing perfectly!

The third reason some people say "No" to God is *they think they are not quite ready.* They have projects that they have not started, projects that are half finished, telephone calls to make, unanswered letters to write. When they get their desks cleared and have a chance to think, probably then they will turn to God. But right now they are just too busy.

The trouble is, there may not be a "later on." Do it now! Do not let God wait. If you feel a positive, inspiring thought go through your mind today, there is only one way to answer it: "Yes, Lord."

Say it now. It is not going to hurt you. Right now, lay this book on your lap and say the words, "Yes, Lord." Repeat them out loud until they sound natural. "Yes, Lord! Yes, Lord! Yes, Lord!"

Do not be afraid of seeming overly dramatic or of being overly emotional; do not let any negative fear hold you back. Say it strongly, positively: "Yes, Lord," I predict that within an hour a positive thought will come into your mind. A positive mood will begin to creep over you. When that happens, do not say, "No." Say again, "Yes, Lord."

THE GOOD NEWS

The good news is that God has promised us that any person who wants salvation can have it. And when that happens, Jesus Christ will come into our lives and make a permanent alteration that will irreversibly, divinely transform our deepest character so that we shall never live a life of self-denigration which leads to decadence and depravity. Rather, our life will reflect beauty, glory, honor, and dignity. Christ within us will help develop our innermost potential for good in such a way that, through the pursuit of our God-given possibilities, we will become the person He wants us to be. Again, there is a superb amplification of this thought in a line from Cardinal Karol Wojytla's (Pope John Paul II) writings, "the glory of God is living man; the glory of God is man alive. And God also leads man to glory."

YOU ARE WONDERFUL WHEN…

BY CARING FOR OTHERS, YOU LET GOD'S LOVE SHINE!

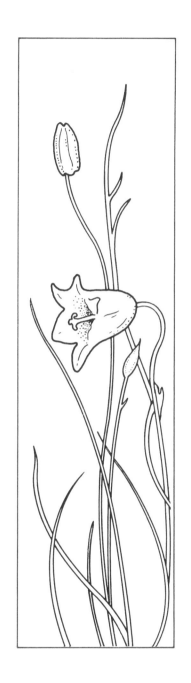

HEAVEN IS SHARING AND CARING

The *prescription* for joyful living is very simple: If you want to be happy, treat people right. If you carry somebody else's burdens, in the process you'll discover the secret of happiness.

There is a story of a man who had a dream one night. He dreamed that he died and found himself immediately in a large room. In the room there was a huge banquet table filled with all sorts of delicious food. Around the banquet table were people seated on chairs, obviously hungry. But the chairs were five feet from the edge of the table and the people apparently could not get out of the chairs. Furthermore, their arms were not long enough to reach the food on the table.

In the dream there was one single large spoon, five feet long. Everyone was fighting, quarreling, pushing each other, trying to grab hold of that spoon. Finally, in an awful scene, one strong bully got hold of the spoon. He reached out, picked up some food, and turned it to feed himself, only to find that the spoon was so long that as he held it out he could not touch his mouth. The food fell off.

Immediately, someone else grabbed the spoon. Again, the person reached far enough to pick up the food, but he could not feed himself. The handle was too long.

In the dream, the man who was observing it all said to his guide, "This is hell—to have food and not be able to eat it."

The guide replied, "Where do you think you are? This is hell. But this is not your place. Come with me."

And they went into another room. In this room there was also a long table filled with food, exactly as in the other room. Everyone was seated in chairs, and for some reason they, too, seemed unable to get out of their chairs.

Like the others, they were unable to reach the food on the table. Yet they had a satisfied, pleasant look on their faces. Only then did the visitor see the reason why. Exactly as before, there was only one spoon. It, too, had a handle five feet long. Yet no one was fighting for it. In fact, one man, who held the handle, reached out, picked up the food, and put it into the mouth of someone else, who ate it and was satisfied.

That person then took the spoon by the handle, reached for the food from the table, and put it back to the mouth of the man who had just given him something to eat. And the guide said, "This is heaven."

YOU'RE NOT AN ISLAND!

"I Need Help!"

"I've got a problem—can you help me?"

"I don't understand—can you enlighten me?"

"I can't agree with you—can we meet somewhere in the middle?"

"I've got a problem accepting this—can you give a little from your position?"

"I'm really at a loss—can you direct me?"

"I'm ready to quit—what is your advice?"

"I'm at my wits' end! I've had it—Please tell me what you think I should do."

These forthright confessions are the beginning of a new beginning! Let's examine the miracle power available to us when we learn to say, "I need help."

If you feel trapped, lost, out-of-control, chained by difficulties, then I have good news for you. *Your chains can lead to a change* if you are willing to say these three words.

Blessed are those who know what it is that they do not know, and who are eager to listen to others who are older, wiser, more experienced. Blessed indeed are they who, in true meekness, remember that a little learning is a dangerous thing. Blessed are those who never forget they are never too old to learn. They shall inherit great wisdom and, with it, success.

WE NEED TO HAVE A NEED

I remember years ago, when E. Stanley Jones used to conduct "ashrams" as he called them. An ashram is a term from India. It means a time of spiritual growth and expansion. Dr. Jones always began his ashrams by passing out pieces of paper and saying, "No one will see what you are about to write on this paper. I want you to write what your need is today."

It happened at every ashram. While people were thinking and praying and writing, someone would say, "Brother Stanley, I don't have a need. What do you write down if you don't have a need?" And Brother Stanley would say, "If you think you don't have a need, then *that's* your need!"

"I'M NOT PERFECT"

Only deeply secure people with a strong, positive self-image dare to admit that they too need to grow and change. Only the person with a healthy self-esteem dares to admit "I'm not perfect. I need to make changes somewhere in my system." By contrast inwardly insecure persons do not dare to ask dangerous questions which threaten their own well-established traditional positions. This may explain why it is difficult for some people who have reached professional prominence to admit, "I was wrong." "I still have much to learn." "I have my own blind spots." "I have areas in my own thought system where I need to grow." "I am more interested in being right than in being applauded by my peers, my students, my colleagues, my supporters, and my cohorts."

WHAT IS GOD TRYING TO DO?

What is God trying to do in this world of ours? I believe He is trying to build a society of human beings who live out the golden rule, "Do unto others as you would have them do unto you." In modern, understandable language this means: Treat each person with dignity and respect.

This means that the kingdom of God is that invisible collection of committed Christians that transcends cultures, ideologies, nationalistic prejudices, and creeds—all bound by the golden commitment to say nothing and do nothing that would attack the self-esteem, the self-respect, and the dignity of any other human being, whether or not they are committed members of the kingdom of God. The dignity of the person then is the irreducible cell of true Christianity.

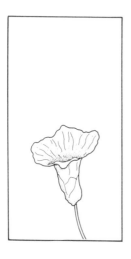

HOW WILL HE SUCCEED?

Now, we turn to another question, how in the world does God hope to succeed? "By His power." What is that? In a word, it is Christ. This is the message the church has to proclaim. It is our witness to the world. By Christ we are delivered from fear to love. We dare to love people. We are inwardly secure enough to treat everyone with respect and dignity. As such, we are not lacking in confidence so that we have to threaten, intimidate, manipulate, dominate, control or victimize others. Christ is our living personal friend. We are His precious associate in service, so we need not seek earthly recognition. We are delivered from vain ego trips and do not need to be a name dropper. All other human connections, compliments, and credits pale into insignificance alongside the glory of being Christ's personal friend and ambassador.

Because of this, our self-image is dynamically positive, for we sense that Christ's love is flowing through us. His Holy Spirit is assuring us of our infinite worth and dignity in His sight as we allow ourselves to be the healing channel of Christ's nonjudgmental love. Now we see all other persons as the children of God whom Christ loves and into whose lives He would love to dwell with grace and truth and honor.

PARDON THOSE WHO HAVE HURT YOU

"Not easy," you say. And you are right. One of the most difficult things to do is to forgive someone who has hurt you. Again, we take a lesson from Jesus in dealing positively with our persecution.

When He was on the cross, stripped of His dignity, Jesus cried out, "Father, forgive them, for they know not what they do!"

Sometimes it is *humanly* impossible to forgive. When that happens, we need to call upon divine intervention. We ask God to forgive those who hurt us and to work on our hearts so that we can eventually see our hurt from their perspective.

Frequently, more often than not, people who hurt others through their words or their actions are unaware that they've injured anybody. They "know not what they do" in terms of being so mixed up, so troubled, so spiteful, or so insecure that they act purely out of gut instinct. They are incapable of thinking about others' feelings or others' lives.

Take humble pride in this: only the of-
fended can forgive. The guilty cannot ex-
tend pardon. By offering reconciliation,
we are set apart as the least sinful. We
move from the defensive to the offensive.
We rise from the role of soldier to the role
of statesman. We become compatible in-
stead of combatable.

GIVERS ARE WINNERS!

John Crean was living in a state of spiritual and economic poverty when a wise friend said to him, "John, there are two kinds of people—losers and winners, takers and givers. Takers are losers; givers are winners. If you want to win, you have to stop taking and start giving. Give more to your boss on the job; give more than is expected from you. Then see what happens." It was radical advice, but he followed it. He was noticed and rewarded. John saved enough to start a business "built on the giving, not taking principle." He decided to manufacture a product that would really solve deep human needs—he'd provide job opportunities to persons who could enjoy the pride of earnership. He'd offer a financial package so poor people could afford to buy and enjoy the pride of ownership.

The result is history. He succeeded and became financially independent and wealthy. Now, he has just given thirty percent of his capital base toward development of a retreat and renewal center where the poorest of the poor can find freedom from their oppression. And who are the poorest of the poor? They are people who have lost all faith in themselves, in the positive potential of society in God, and in their fellow-man.

Here is a fundamental rule of life: If you want people to treat you nicely, treat them nicely. For every action, there is a reaction. For every positive action, there is a positive reaction. For every negative action, there is a negative reaction.

ACCEPT YOURSELF...
ACCEPT OTHERS

If you want to treat people mercifully, you have to begin by treating yourself mercifully. Accept yourself by knowing that Christ accepts you just as you are! However, if you lack a deep inner sense of self-esteem and self-worth, you will constantly have problems with other people. You won't treat them mercifully. You'll be unkind. You'll be critical or you'll gossip. You'll lash back until you've undermined the most important aspects of your life—and you find it collapsed around you.

Think about it. What is it that keeps us from treating people mercifully? It's resentment, jealousy, or the feeling that someone is a threat to you. If you can't handle resentment, jealousy, or "victimitis," then deep down in your own mind, heart, and soul you need to deal with your lack of a positive self-image. Your negative reactions are the result of hidden wounds that need to be healed.

"GOD LOVES YOU AND SO DO I"

"God loves you and so do I" is more than just a slogan. It is a proud, positive proclamation of the Cross—the vertical and the horizontal intersection of a relationship with God and a relationship with those around me. The Cross is the divine-human intersection. God gives my self-respect a boost with His nonjudgmental love. I must do the same for my fellow humans. I must get involved. I must accept the dream God gives me and develop its inherent possibilities.

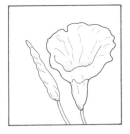

KIND PEOPLE

The kind people are the sensitive spirits. They are the quiet people, through whom God can do so much. They are also those who are *willing to be third.* Happy, indeed, are the people who are willing to put Jesus first, others second, and themselves third in line. Richly rewarded in this life are those who learn the lesson of our Lord that if any man would be master, he should learn to be a servant.

In summary, what is the kingdom of God? It is a community of caring and Christ-inspired, compassionate people, who are committed to building a self-respecting society of persons whose inalienable right to self-worth controls communication, evangelism, economics, social ethics, and political systems.

YOU ARE WONDERFUL BECAUSE…

GOD HAS GIVEN YOU A SPECIAL DREAM!

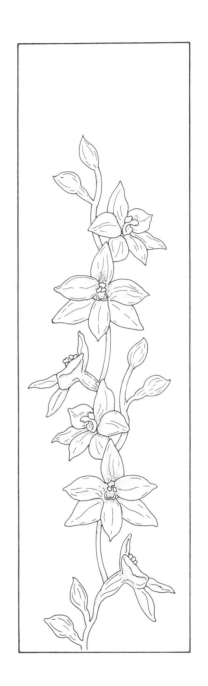

THREE PENNIES AND A DREAM

Mother Teresa of Calcutta had a dream. She told her superiors, "I have three pennies and a dream from God to build an orphanage."

"Mother Teresa," her superiors chided gently, "you cannot build an orphanage with three pennies. With three pennies, you can't do anything."

"I know," she said, smiling, "but with God and three pennies I can do anything!"

Mother Teresa has become an international symbol of real success.

But, what is ultimate success? I hold that success is experiencing the self-esteem that arises deep within us when we build it in others through sincere self-denial and sacrificial service. To build self-esteem in others is to walk in God's will and do His work. To build self-worth in another person is the fulfillment of the prayer, "Thy kingdom come, thy will be done."

GO FOR IT!

Are you satisfied? Are you happy? Is life all that you hoped it would be? It can be—it *will* be—if you will say "Yes" to the dream that God has given you.

Go for it! You might make it!

Go for it! It might happen!

Go for it! Somebody might be helped by it!

Go for it! You might rise from poverty to prosperity!

Go for it! If you prosper, you might be able to help the poor!

Go for it! Someday, somebody will come to you and say, "Thank you!"

"GOOD PEOPLE ARE HAPPY"

I once asked Dr. Joyce Brothers, the well-known psychologist, "Joyce, what are some of the most basic, deepest psychological needs that you see in human beings today?"

She replied, "I think that human beings need *love*. It doesn't have to be the love between a man and a woman. It can be love of mankind. It can be love of God. William James said it so many years ago: 'The most important thing in life is to *live your life for something more important than your life.*' That's what happy people do.

"You know, we live in an age of miracle drugs," Dr. Brothers continued, "But the miracle that still does the most to lengthen life, to make it happy, is the oldest miracle we know. It is the miracle of love. And from a psychologist's point of view, I see that people who are good are happy. People who are happy are people who are good.

"Human beings are capable of so much. Again, psychologists have found that people use only ten percent of their ability. But there are some people who will not stop at that ten percent. They push the limits, to find out what they are capable of doing. Those are the happy people."

GOD KNOWS YOU TRIED

Righteousness is attempting to accomplish some beautiful possibility. Win or lose—the attempt will build your self-esteem. Succeed or fail—you can be sure of this—you will be able to live with yourself and not be ashamed, which means you can be proud that you tried.

That's the joy! That's the deep satisfaction! That is the great reward!

DARE TO DREAM GREAT DREAMS!

We can begin to see the positive enthusiasm-generating, depression-dispelling power on this command of Christ, "If anyone would come after me, he must deny himself and take up his cross and follow me:" (Matt. 16:24).

"...And follow me"? What does that mean? It means daring to dream a great dream!

Divine dreams are the tap roots of enthusiasm. So, we are called to join God's kingdom. You and I are called to be modern disciples of Jesus. We are called to think of the possibilities God has for us. We are called to deny ourselves, take up our cross, and follow Him.

THE DAY LEONARDO DA VINCI COULDN'T PAINT

I love a story I once heard about Leonardo da Vinci. According to the legend, some lads were visiting the famous artist. One of them knocked over a stack of canvases. This upset the artist because he was working very quietly and sensitively. He became angry, threw his brush, and hurled some harsh words to the hapless little fellow, who ran crying from the studio.

The artist was now alone again, and he tried to continue his work. He was trying to paint the face of Jesus, but he couldn't do it. His creativity had stopped.

Leonardo da Vinci put down his brush. He went out and walked the streets and the alleys until he found the little boy. He said, "I'm sorry, son; I shouldn't have spoken so harshly. Forgive me, even as Christ forgives. I have done something worse than you. You only knocked over the canvases. But I, by my anger, blocked the flow of God into my life. Will you come back with me?"

He took the boy back into the studio with him. They smiled as the face of Jesus came quite naturally from the master's brush. That face has been an inspiration to millions ever since.

Righteousness?
It is:
positive,
Faith-Producing
people
who are actively
pursuing
a God-given
dream!

Blessed are the honest, hardworking folks. They are more interested in substance than in style. They are more concerned about character building than about popularity rating. They are more dedicated to making solid achievements than to running after swift but synthetic happiness.

MAKE PEOPLE BELIEVE IN YOU!

There is a success principal that I call the laminated principle. It works like this: You make a promise—and deliver. You accept an assignment—and fulfill it. You attempt something "impossible"—and pull it off. Finally, year after year, maybe decade after decade, you have applied one accomplishment on top of another, one achievement over another—promises kept and commitments fulfilled. Your reputation is like a laminated beam that has durability and power. People believe in you. They take you at your word. They'll sign a contract with you because they know you're going to deliver. Blessed are the patient people, blessed are the persistent. They shall ultimately win.

STRAIGHT AHEAD!

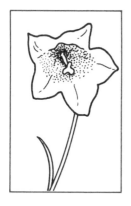

Let me share with you one of the most inspiring sights that I've ever seen. It happened on the slopes of Squaw Valley. The handicapped skier's name was Kim Caulfield. She was about eighteen and blind. Kim was being led down the giant slalom. She made it through forty-four gates, and she was lined up straight with the finish line. Her guide behind her said, "Straight ahead Kim; go for it!"

Kim dug in and was flying over the snow when she hit a rut. The poles flew out of her hands. She fell flat on her stomach. She knew she'd have to get her body across the finish line or be disqualified. She looked beaten, but she didn't stop. She reached out for her poles. When she couldn't find them, she started swimming over the snow, straight ahead, until she crossed the finish line.

"Kim, you made it!" the judge called out. But she didn't hear him. She just kept swimming over the snow flat on her stomach for another five–ten–fifteen feet.

DOES SUCCESS ALONE SATISFY?

Fame doesn't satisfy. Neither does success. Tom Landry, the super-successful coach of the Dallas Cowboys, is successful. But more than that, he is *satisfied*. Surprisingly, he shared with me that his satisfaction doesn't come merely from winning football games, although he does feel it's important to try with all our might to be all that we can be.

In fact, Tom said that there is a slogan he keeps prominently displayed in the Cowboys' locker room: "The quality of a person's life is in direct proportion to his commitment to excellence." Tom went on to say, "I believe that very strongly. I believe that God gave us all talent to do whatever we want to do and He expects us to do the best we can. When you try to be the best you can, then success and winning take care of themselves.

"Confidence comes from knowledge. If you know your job well, then you'll have the confidence to do it well when you get out on the field. You've got to anticipate the positive element all the time, because once you start thinking about the negative possibilities—that you may miss the Super Bowl, or you may lose, you may be fired next week—such negative thinking drastically reduces your chances of achieving your best. And so we try to think positively."

Tom Landry is a success. He says that anybody can be a winner if he wants it bad enough, strives for it hard enough, actively seeks it out by learning all he can and working with all his strength. Of course, positive anticipation, feeding on good, clear, positive attitudes is essential.

WHAT IF I FAIL?

What if God gives me a noble dream, a high calling, and *I find I don't have what it takes?* Will I succeed or fail? Is success important? Yes, it is terribly important. For nothing is more destructive to a person's self-esteem than the fear of being a terrible failure! If the church genuinely cares about a person's total life, we will do all we can to lead and lift every person into self-affirming experiences. Self-affirmation is success. God, who deals with our inferiority, will handle our anxiety over success and failure, too.

> Passionate persistence
> without impertinence
> produces progress!

"IT'S WHAT'S INSIDE THAT COUNTS"

In the book, *Gone with the Wind,* we read about the Southern gentleman who broke down under the tragedies involved in the Civil War. Observing his collapse, another character in the novel philosophizes, "He could be licked from the inside. I mean to say that what the world could not do, his own heart could." Then the simple philosopher concluded, "There ain't anything from the outside that can lick any of us."

YOU ARE
WONDERFUL
WHEN…

YOU ACCEPT
GOD AS
YOUR REFUGE
AND YOUR
STRENGTH!

"I HAVE CALLED YOU BY NAME"

Christianity isn't a Pollyanna religion. It doesn't claim that bad things won't happen to us. We are never told in the Old or New Testament that if we live a good life we'll never have any sickness or tragedy. However, we are promised in Isaiah 43 (1-3): "Fear not, for I have redeemed you; I have called you by name, you are mine. When you pass through the waters...they shall not overwhelm you; when you walk through fire you shall not be burned, and the flame shall not consume you. For I am the Lord your God."

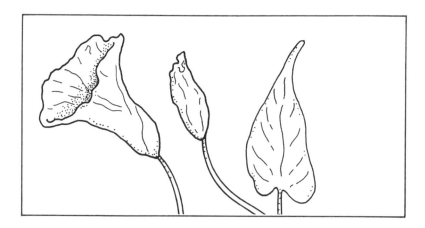

GOD GIVES US A SENSE OF CALM

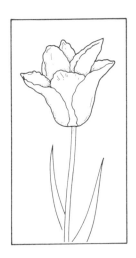

How does God comfort people when bad things happen to them? He gives them courage. He also gives them a sense of calm—in the most unexpected times and ways. As it is said in an old Christian hymn, "Sometimes the light surprises a Christian while he sings; it is the Lord who comes with healing on His wings."

I recall the sister of the late congressman, Clyde Doyle. She had two children, a son and a daughter. Both of them were killed when they were teenagers. Her husband also died at a fairly early age. She was completely alone. You know, it's easy to go to someone and say, "Don't look at what you have lost, look at what you still have." But here was a woman who had no one left!

I asked, "Where did you find comfort? What gives you the strength to keep going?"

She said, "I live in Long Beach. I used to go to the beach every day. Often I just sat there numb. I could not think, I could not feel, but I could still see. And I watched the waves as they built into a curl of foam, as they washed up onto the sand and then retreated. I did that day after day, week after week, month after month, and year after year. One day, as I watched the wave curl, break, foam, and sweep across the sand, I was struck with a message from God. I heard a voice within me say, 'There is nothing but life!'"

And she said, "I knew then where my son was! I knew where my daughter was, and where my husband was!" For the first time, she was able to feel a sense of peace. And then she was able to start building her life again.

TAKE ONE STEP FURTHER

Worry, anxiety, pressures, frustrations—all of these can cause us to be blinded to the real world all around us. When we take this one step further, you can see how easy it would be for some emotional blockage to keep us from being aware of the presence of God.

"Blessed are the pure in heart, for they shall see God." I believe Jesus is teaching that if we have emotional and spiritual health we will be able to "see" God, to believe in Him.

It is possible! No matter how great, how deep, how bitter the suffering—when we turn our trials over to Jesus, He can turn them into triumphs! He can do the impossible. He can work miracles. And He can carry us through the phases of collision and withdrawal into the healing phase of acceptance, if we but let Him.

What is this pain?
It is the birth pang
of a new attitude
trying to be born!

"Attitudes are more important than facts!"

Karl Menninger

Linda Down, a victim of cerebral palsy, ran an entire marathon, and she's inspired millions! She's found the secret of happiness. What is it? It's her attitude—"If I attempt the impossible in my condition, perhaps I can inspire others to be happy and successful too."

BY PAIN WE CAN GROW

I count it an honor to call Art Linkletter a friend. His humor and delightful way of looking at American life have brought joy and laughter into all of our lives. But when you look beyond Art's wit and optimism you see a man who has turned his cross into a commission—a commitment to reach the lives of young people who are ensnared in the deathtrap of drugs. All of this grew out of his daughter's tragic death as a result of drugs and his son's death in an automobile accident.

I asked him once, "Art, how do you turn a tragedy into a personal triumph?"

He answered me in his warm, wise, loving manner, "The most difficult thing is to admit the tragedy, to accept it. It is something in your life over which you had no control, and God's plan for us, as we all know, is more than we can fathom. It's part of the pattern of life—life and death.

"Having once admitted and accepted the deep, deep pain of the wound, then you begin to realize that you have expanded your own capability of loving and caring for others. Until you are hurt, you can never truly understand the hurts of others. Until you have failed, you cannot truly achieve success. In my own case, the pain in my life started me on a crusade against drug abuse—trying to help young people and families.

"Not everybody may be called to start a crusade as I was, but everyone can reflect love and caring. Every person's life touches some other life that needs love today."

PERSIST IN TRUSTING GOD

When we are suffering, it is tempting to lash out at everyone around us—including God. And it is hard to keep on trusting Him when we are being rejected or ridiculed. But if we are to be victorious in the face of persecution, it is vital to maintain our trust in Him.

The Book of Job has been hailed by students of literature as one of the greatest epic poems ever written. But it is far more than a beautiful piece of literature. Job is a story of triumphal trust—for surely nobody has ever faced more persecution than Job.

"When he has tried me, I shall come forth as gold" (Job 23:10).

"Though he slay me, yet will I trust in him" (Job 13:15).

Both of these statements made by Job *after* he faced persecution are testimonial to the fact that he successfully endured his persecution. Job illustrates a faith that will not lose its grip, a faith that never lets go.

Let's examine Job's trials. He was very rich. He had three thousand camels, which would be like having a few hundred Rolls-Royces today. He had seven sons and three daughters. His fame was worldwide. He was what you could call super-rich, super-successful. At the age of thirty-nine, he had it made. And on top of everything, he had a reputation for being religious.

One day, according to the book of Job, the devil appeared to the Almighty and said, "So, you think Job's such a good guy? Let me tell you—it is easy to have faith when you're rich like that. The truth is that Job only comes across with a smiling, happy faith because life is easy for him. He's rich. But if he were poor and suffering, then we'd see what kind of faith Job really has."

In this epic poem God agrees that the devil can try Job. The first thing that happens to him is financial ruin. He loses all of his property. The next thing that happens is that his house collapses and all of his children are killed. Then once the money is gone, Job's opportunistic friends go. He's lost his money, his family, and his power; the community just doesn't respond to him anymore. Finally one day he sits in the ashes, naked. And he says, "Naked I came from my mother's womb, and naked shall I return; the Lord gave, and the Lord has taken away; blessed be the name of the Lord" (Job 1:21).

Then he adds this inspiring pledge:

"When he has tried me, I shall come forth as gold!"

We were designed to breathe in faith and exhale cynicism. In our natural emotional habitat and healthy state of mind, we were created to be trusting persons.

DON'T PRETEND

Poverty handled in a pleasant, positive manner is an opportunity to involve good and generous people in our dreams, for often the strong welcome an opportunity to help the weak. The wealthy find meaning in their lives when they are given an opportunity to share in some worthy project or person. Today I enjoy the friendship of many wonderful people whom I met when I had to beg for their help to build a Crystal Cathedral or to spread a ministry via television.

I have been blessed because I have been poor—poor enough to swallow my pride and humbly ask for assistance. The result? Not merely success in reaching my occupational goals, but lasting friendships with those who saved the day for me.

So, don't become defensive about your lack by trying to gloss over it or pretending the problem doesn't exist.

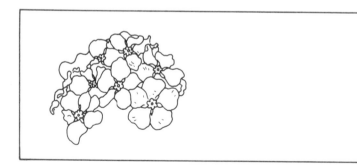

THE PROMISE

Throughout the Scriptures God promises that He will be merciful to us:

"His *mercy* is on those who fear (trust) him" (Luke 1:50).

"God, who is rich in *mercy*, out of the great love with which he loved us...made us alive together with Christ" (Eph. 2:4,6).

"He saved us, not because of deeds done by us in righteousness, but in virtue of his own *mercy*" (Titus 3:5).

The promise is there! It is for *you!* What wonderful news! What wonderful assurance! No matter where our road will lead, no matter what pain may hit, no matter what we do, God will be there with His mercy to forgive us, to hold us up, and carry us through the tough times.

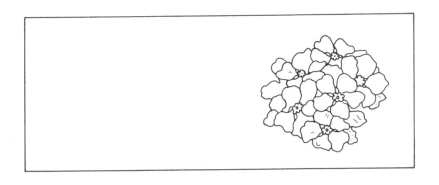

Edited by Stephanie C. Oda
Book design by Holly Johnson
Typeset in Zapf Chancery Bold and Bembo
Cover design by Robert Pantelone
Cover photograph by Joseph A. DiChello, Jr.